Hours of the Cardinal

THE
James
DICKEY
CONTEMPORARY POETRY SERIES

EDITED BY RICHARD HOWARD

Hours of the Cardinal

Poems by
RICHARD LYONS

University of South Carolina Press

Published in Columbia, South Carolina, by the
University of South Carolina Press

Manufactured in the United States of America

04 03 02 01 00   5 4 3 2 1

Library of Congress Cataloging-in-Publication Data

Lyons, Richard, 1951–
  Hours of the cardinal / Richard Lyons.
    p. cm. — (The James Dickey contemporary poetry series)
  ISBN 1-57003-320-X (alk. paper)
  ISBN 1-57003-321-8 (pbk. : alk. paper)
  I. Title. II. Series.
  PS3562.Y4494 H68 2000
  811'.54—dc21   99-050777

Acknowledgment is made to the editors of the following publications, where some of the poems included here originally appeared, sometimes in slightly different form: *Crazyhorse,* "In Defense of the Body," "A Half Inch of Blue Sky," "Some Weeks before an Autumn Wedding"; *Gettysburg Review,* "The Thousands of Little Fires," "An Address to Marina Tsvetayeva Curling Inward"; *Gulf Coast Review,* "Blue Exorcism"; *Indiana Review,* "Hours of the Cardinal"; *New Republic,* "Charon's Boat"; *North American Review,* "Blackout"; *Paris Review,* "Vantage Point," "Archaic Smile," "Stanzas Written at Baba Yaga's," "The Black Venus: For Max Ernst," "Symmetry," "The Corpse Washing"; *Passages North,* "For Dianne Wherever She May Be," "Like Glass Pyramids at Midnight"; *Western Humanities Review,* "Summer: Silver Flashing," "Morning: Merrymeeting Lake," "Two Deaths in San Bernardino," "In an Instant."

The author offers special thanks to Bill Kerley, Gary Myers, Bill Olsen, Nancy Eimers, and Dave Wojahn.

NATIONAL
ENDOWMENT
FOR THE ARTS

Publication of this book was supported by a grant from the National Endowment for the Arts.

For Leah

Through the first gate,
Into our first world, shall we follow
The deception of the thrush? Into our first world.
T. S. ELIOT

If love does a secret thing always, it is to reach
backward, to a time that could not be known.
EUDORA WELTY

What did your face look like
before your father and mother met?
ZEN KOAN

Contents

A Note on Richard Lyons

as if all of this would go up in flames
against black water

Laudable the decorum, amid some of the most sumptuous evidence in contemporary practice, of this poet's technical moderation: here are few or none of the regulation devices in the art's armory, means to overpower and literally captivate a reader rendered helpless by the blessed potencies of meter and rhyme, of alliterative chime and predictable rite. This poet owns up to a certain diffidence, perhaps not immediately located among so much that is exultant and in-your-face, as we curiously say nowadays; he manifests a certain reluctance when it comes to pulling out all the stops. Richard Lyons invokes but two, the *vox humana* and a resonance of wisdom, of that aphorismic utterance that Bacon called "a wisdom broken." Other poetic contraptions he eschews, and that is his modesty, his reticence: to insist on such splendor out of such headlong and demotic makings:

> . . . The sun smites

> everything its blindness touches.
> This is the beginning of God: erasure & accrual.

Repeatedly, this will be his method, or at least his madness: to elegize (the book is one long script or scrawl of mourning for his late mother) even as he exults, a raving continually brought up short by riven judgments, split hairs. "Yes," he addresses Tsvetayeva ("curling inward"), "Marina, we will ride along like this after death, / a part of everything except ourselves"—the moving extravagance succeeded immediately by the driest of verities. And all the rest is landscape and closely reckoned scenic observation, the details of an unparalleled exuberance among the things of this world:

> watching the lettering of our names break up like leaf cinders wafting a few feet namelessly attached to the air,

> just one more iridescent feather beginning the day outside alien as it is, dear latecomer,

> dear self, a bit of light from winter's harsh candle.

Lyons has deepened his register since a first collection, *These Modern Nights,* some years back, and I venture to say that loss has sweetened his throat like a lozenge; Rilke is the only other mourner I know whose laments, not even so much as these, sound the entire range of ecstatic apprehension. There is of course the odd Whitmanian resonance—if I name it so, maybe it will help the reader locate the functional *Stimmung* more readily—the sort of narcissistic eros that we so quickly identify as a Song of Myself:

> Happiness is a plausible aesthetic, isn't it?

> I walk out among the thorn trees
> and spot a thatch of goat's hair on a low branch.
> I am by myself, owed nothing by anyone, my accurate accounts.

> The blast furnace of the sky!

> What do I owe
>   when each breath is a betrayal, each day
> passing me on in smaller & smaller strips?

> I don't rummage in another life for whatever I've done—

And of course there are the direct references to all the poets, from Vaughan to Tu Fu, who pledge allegiance to—or alignment with—the changing earth. But they are references only, the swiftest of allusions in the rapt garrulity of these chants, which must set up a certain length, a certain breadth, in order for the marvelous simplicities to *set in*. Have but a little patience with the unsupported (as by the rigmarole of prosody) palaver of it all, to use a cherished Lyons word as you will hear in a second, and it is my privilege to promise an overtaken reader the greatest sum of exorbitance, sublimity, and dole in all the American poetry of our worst century's end; how else to call such expression:

> *We push the boat from shore*
> *with the sucking sound of mud.*
>
> *Several black & white buffle-head ducks break from the water.*
>
> *Then all is quiet.*
> *In the distance a waterfall, like a rope in thin air,*
>
> *drops its palaver.*
>
> *Our tongues, old boats, rot in the coves of our mouths.*
> *Bees breed in the white poppies,*
> *they fill the chalk fissures with sun.*
> *The earth is gentle, the river speeding on.*

Modest, then, is my word for this withdrawn poet who creates such things, such raptures, without once raising or rounding his voice. It is the mystery of a new sublime, and Lyons is its master.

RICHARD HOWARD

Hours of the Cardinal

Morning, Merrymeeting Lake

This is the summer of our superfluity,
our bikes ditched.
The Green Mountains a burnished sort of brown.

As I look back, we're climbing a ridge,

already August, the mottled tops of the trees
swirling around the way, after Labor Day,
school life will: lockers slammed, books, Biology's frog
                                      suspended in clear solution.
Each step we take is a soft one
across lung-colored or wasp-colored leaves.
We're wearing yellow baseball caps with the letters
      A - E - R - I - A - L   L - I - F - T
stitched on the hairline. These hieroglyphs,

if they mean anything, mean something to your brother
whose gawky free advertisement we are

up & down the ten or twelve blocks back home,

Mickey, Hank & a utility outfielder whose name escapes me,
all flapping against the spokes of our Schwinns.
Schwinn, the word itself makes me resay it,

pushing the ball bearing of my tongue back
for the vowel—the rush of breath a little wind
making it perfect: *Schwinn* . . . making us as swift

1

as Moorish pirates on horseback, scything the air with scimitars.
Schwinn . . . . We mistrust the law behind what can't be seen,
the bobcat's ghostly soft striding gesture of refusal to sit still.

Wild hunters, we're shy like them—
they're part of what we imagine, like the girls at the Mall
undressing the alabaster bodies of mannequins,
                              wigs like golfers' divots on the floor.
Now sunlight slips through the leaves the way cheese does
through a slicer, each particular plane of light.

We toss rocks at crows smoothing their shiny wings.
We wave our caps across the mouths of caves,
                              papier-mâché torsos of dead leaves.
By noon we can make out in the distance
                         the inlet of East Merrymeeting
where, for all it's worth & all we know, the bobcat hides—
                         face pushed in, whiskers flared—
not wanting to hurt anyone, least of all two boys
who know so little they're ghosts themselves.

All in one motion, the trees lift their silly hats
to the sheer unreflective height of day.

I

Charon's Boat

AFTER PATINIER

This is the sort of light
in which there are the two of us

focused, for a moment, on the fiery leaf of a man
poling his boat from one shore to the other

where beasts, as final & etched as birth,
sleep near the mouth of a watery underground palace.

From some chink in the foundation
the glare of a fire traces each leaf,

each particular red-veined deliquescence,
as if each added to each composed an odyssey

and not the shuttle of a ferry across the water.
Now, each life of his, each journey,

is passengerless, so this is the end, endlessly rehearsed.
Gnarled souls no longer tumble into the abyss.

No one floats into the fiery perspective of the sky.
The man keeps his leaf of a boat on the lick of a wave,

arms arced back as if to shove the boat forward,
but he's wavering, pushing the hair & beard away.

Each undulation, each lick & curl, keeps us
at a distance, which is aesthetic, thus a stalled

way of seeing: one shore of estuary & white mosaic,
one dark necessary citadel that draws us on.

The Thousands of Little Fires

On all sides are ghosts, not of the dead,
but of living people.
SHERWOOD ANDERSON

The dead must have tipped their parched tongues
to the barbed thistle & the mica
               when the angel shattered the rock over hell.
They must have laid their soft melon heads on the ground
like this: cheeks pocked with pebbles & seashells,
the chill nightdew on their foreheads, on ours—

a fever broken. They must have heard the same
humiliating cocksure music of constellations:
fire, dust & indivisible specks of blood.

The dead don't go away, they disappear.

                         On nights like these
they pinch a wrist between thumb & forefinger,
                         a cold, concentrated burn.
They look like, of all things, bashed veins of beryl & tourmaline.
They share each cold lost breath the living breathe.

───────────

If I had anything more than the clothes on my back
I can't recall what it was

or if I ever wanted it.
In these moon craters
the cactus wrens wheedle cover wherever they may:
their not being particular a precise bob & weave.

Dave is cleaning a pot of beans.
I hear him rub the sides with sand.
A few men sit under a tree & laugh among themselves.

The hills lean away, bald & easily unpretentious.
Like the men, they desire only to breathe inside their skins
a few hundred years more.

I think of the hermit saint everywhere in the bright expanse of rock.
I think of the blond dust of ancient comets in his hair.

I peel one small pearl-white onion & sprinkle it over eggs
spitting above the blue jet from the Coleman. The sun smites

everything its blindness touches.
This is the beginning of God: erasure & accrual.

———————

In the roseate fingers of dawn,
                    blood-speckled & tired,
the local economy awakens: hawkers, they know who we are:
the zinc-glitter of comet dust on our shoes.

Later, we devour hot torpedoes of green corn
and brown lumps of sugar.

A man whose name he says is Jesse
wheels a boot-black throne to the next turn.

Our dusty loafers, a dollar apiece, if Jesse guesses
what street "you got them on."

You're here, he says, you got them on Calle Rosa, he laughs,
wielding one arm toward an arch
where a large blue sign flashes on & off.

———————

With Dave, I can be as small as I want to be.

I can curse, fuss, even color the buff-brown mirror
of contorted crucifixes with the white flecks of thought.
I'm wondering

if Stendhal's mirror mounted on the back of a wagon
in the woods outside Paris could forget
all we must forget to enter the aesthetics of sand,

all we must love on the red-rimmed hills of this planet,
                                         this bitter rose.
As Dave tips the van at top speed, I'm talking about another
one of my endless fantasies for world reconciliation,
the thousands of little fires

closing their angel-wings into one fierce inferno.

Dave says, "Look!" Nine wild horses
bank into the carmine dust of sunset.

———————

Beneath the beaten gold negative of noon

a horse cart rolls slowly down the beach,
medlars & cigar-rolls of cinnamon for sale.

Two boys press them into our hands & demand greenbacks
that blow out to sea like gulls, like leaves,

like conversation whisked out of the mind by concentration.

The woman at the reins shoos away flies.
She hasn't lived ever outside her own cares,
                              which shoo her from hill to pier.
What is inside the body makes her rise every morning,
rouse the boys, thumb worms off windfalls
                    to load them like a stash of gems
and go with two sons to the sea.

Will the beautiful faces of the Guatemalan women
                              blossom in some future all my own?
Will the red & white soccer ball their kids maneuver
between our legs, using the hard ruts in the road,

have anything to do with the sunset I'll watch from an apartment
in New York or Boston, tugs chortling smoke & cutting up the water?

Will the years airbrush us out of any picture?
                              Will the chair
where Dave is now shaving parsnips on the porch
stand forever at its precarious angle
                              the way it does
as he bellows "Satisfaction" along with Jagger on the stereo,
the chair rocking on its back legs? When we come right down

to thinking clearly about the present, what does it owe us,
what does it care, flipping its pages before we've written
                              anything on them,
before we smudge them with brooding silence
                              like the mountains brown with sleep.
The men clatter in from the fields, filling the little kitchen
where Esta is lifting a silver pan from the oven.

The parsnips Dave heaps in a colander
do not ask to live inside their skins for a hundred years.

Young Manuel is washing his hands in the sink.
He hangs a small scythe over the stove—

it rocks itself silent as we pass around a large bowl,
                              loosen our belts & ask for more.

The kids are trundling watermelons
                    across the gritty back of the van.
It thumps & puckers beneath these sweet blimps of water.
Young Manuel drops one in the red dust.

Happiness is a plausible aesthetic, isn't it?

I walk out among the thorn trees
and spot a thatch of goat's hair on a low branch.
I am by myself, owed nothing by anyone, my accurate accounts.

The blast furnace of the sky!

What do I owe
                    when each breath is a betrayal, each day
passing me on in smaller & smaller strips?

I don't rummage in another life for whatever I've done—

I have withheld myself, sure, & grow less sure as the days pass.
I have chalked up hours in low wooden houses,
                              a general middle class of experience
far from the yards where chambermaids lie under the trees,
divvying up the paper & sighing in the deep grass.

With his thumb over the hose, Dave is misting aureoles
over the phlox as we sing hoarse & off-key:
You'll Never Know . . . How Love-ly.

The stars dot the slope of the sky like cattle,
like chips of mica, like whatever they please

in the willful self-consciousness of the sky.

In one sustained croak the tree frogs pull the ripcord
of their throats the way baseball cards, long ago,
                              slapped the spokes of my Schwinn.
What I've left undone, the unaccomplishing life that goes on,
                                        the erasure of the sun.

————————

His kids are gold seeds
                    in the harrowing night clouds
over Sugar Land, Texas, where his ex raises chrysanthemums.

We stop to shovel down burritos.
Around our table the Mexican couples dance
                                    in elegant ruffles.
Their children are married, sitting on the broken veranda
a few yards away.

There's a limit to the depths we drive ourselves to,
each sad tune.

Dave tells me of the girls he dated in Spain, each
named for a Christian virtue, each, now, just a name.

In the morning we will cross the desert.
The swath of stars, now, from a town not on any map,
                              reminds us how deep inside the world
we live our lives. I follow the arc of the Dipper

by following Dave's arm. My memory of picking it out
                              against the black pall of the sky
will be intimately connected to that arm sweeping
the lint & gravel of galaxies to one side.
                              It sows gold seeds.
We even name two stars after ourselves
though we're sure, by tomorrow, we will not find ourselves
                              in the sky.

A woman with a red headband is talking to a woman
                                    with burnt red hair.
Their words float, untranslated, sprinkled with beads,
silver tinsel & thin friable dimes.

In a wall niche a statue of the Virgin beckons sinners,
green phosphorescent six-shooters glued to her torso & train.
It's a ghoulish vigil, a green light we stand in awhile unchanged.

Then I go outside & smell the dust on the yucca,
the wind collecting nothing, touching it all.

The dead disappear, they don't go away.

Inside, Dave weaves over to the jukebox to play a bit of cumbia.
He shuffles clumsily in the arms of the woman
                                    with the burnt red hair.
I must watch all this intensely so as to delay my shifting
salvation of the facts, August 12th,
                        the heat lifting from the bent edge of the day.

———————

All of a sudden (how true, in this instance, the banal cue)
the sky is lit up amber & a voice speaks from the sky.

Ahead, a tan vehicle slows down.
A green one pulls alongside
                        & they ask us, at 60 M.P.H.,
to pull over: two quintessential American guys
sleepy, dirty, & suspicious.

A man in a tan cap sweeps his flashlight between our shoulders
                        then he trains it on Dave's hands.
He wishes us a good night, 3 A.M.,
                        then turns around to ask
if we brought any Mexican fruit across the border: mangos, medlars.

Again he wishes us goodnight, after we say, "No, no mangos, nothing"
and it is almost "nada" that stumbles off my tongue.

Just as suddenly, we're alone, a silent steam rising from the engine.

Just as suddenly, we're alone, a silent steam rising from the engine

as the helicopter's light sweeps over something in the brush.
In the penumbra of its holy dust

I don't know how we arrive at an end, the moment's envelope,
unless it is that the light, even the generous light
of the South, is self-referential—
all the roads blown up, leaked, slipping away.

They arc toward the vastness
which may be ahead, the insects grinding the hours, rubbing them out.

Vantage Point

I keep returning to that window
in the mountains of southern Bavaria.
                                I'm pushing the halves open
to the bright sun on sapphires in the shape of trees.

For the oddest most subjective reasons
the washstand—a porcelain cup—could be a chalice of polished bone

or an old Jew's brittle spine, the body's plumbing.

But of course such vagaries of resemblance don't belong on paper.
Outside my room, a young Turkish chamber boy
rolls bedsheets around his frail black arms.

He's singing to himself in the hard syllables
of my incomprehension a delicate halting song.

For all I know it could be the sound of half-tracks
churning up the gravel on the road outside his home.

For all I know it could be the song of the spider
shearing down the ivory of his father's rib cage.

Behind the boy is a tapestried landscape
that grows up the hall & down the stairway.

In it, horses climb the first jagged cliffs,
            each horse hooded, one dead diamond per forelock.
These might as well be Hannibal's harebrained scheme

to conquer the economy of Venus & Apollo,
                                        the perfect white curves
Carthaginians couldn't begin to imagine till now:
the serrated snow brow of mountain, snowblind mighty forms.

One by one & slowly, loaded with provisions & weapons & food,
the elephants muscle patience along the edge of the world.

O dark homunculus, riding the sky,
is it wonder you coax into that giant ear,
the beast's breath like a windsock in the cold blue Alpine air?

———————

One swath of blue is hoisted above the town
where I'm called "professor" for teaching rules to soldiers.

The radar dish tracks the valley into Austria.

Somewhere, adumbrated in blips on a screen,
are the figures of animals we want or fear to see.

In the distance, skiers trace painless scars on powder.

This is the last thing.
This is the next: the commingling of twilight & fire.
I'm talking to Curt who argues for "strike capability."
The other day, he says, a green helicopter pilot
dropped twelve men: fractured jaw, extended tibia, broken foot. . . .

Mornings when able-bodied men patrol the mountain
—small black shadows across shelves of snow—
I wonder: would all this give way beneath a thought
                        that's slipped the mind, softly & a long way down.

Rockface buttresses snow,
it buoys Hannibal's crack troops across a continent,
it buttresses even time.

But maybe what holds everything up is the light,
the way it loves everything it falls on,
                              each branch, each invisible stone.
Is it my own aloneness I'm looking through
at this, this . . . black dog, this asterisk
                                   throbbing on snow?
It keeps my sight going, in any case, endlessly
across waves of pure, wedding-cake drifts.
Then it tumbles through the ancient blue arms of spruce,
which break its fall. I know, I can
still hear the barking: *catch me, little man,*

                              find the stew bone
your mother, the loving German witch-lady,
gave me for my repertoire of roll-over & fetch,

find the stew bone, little man, in the endless avalanche
of stew bones, in the steamy elephant ossuary of snow.

An Address to Marina Tsvetayeva Curling Inward

I open the book to your morose features
against a background of crude triangles & diamonds
that go on in permutation behind you

as if your head were a rogue moon in an exact universe.
                                        I'm reading
how you took the train overnight from Moscow to Paris,
how your friend said, "I love the Eiffel Tower,

it's the one place from which you can't see it."

I'm trying to synchronize my pulse with the pulse
in my mother's thin wrist, the blue & red sinews.

But we are the absence of body.

Your mother, like mine, demanded from you—herself.
Though I tried, in turn, to shape her in my own ghostly image,

as gods do, with the arrogance & vulnerability of best intentions,
she knew the body's imperfections were all we get.

Inside my skull
I expect you to light a candle, elaborating the world's light.

Suddenly we're in a cemetery,
an icy brook of melted snow clear as alcohol.

Is this Elabuga where you decided poems stink?

After my mother's funeral
I crawled back through the sickening sweetness
of blossoming rhododendrons.

I wanted to be alone with my mother.
I was alone.

————

Yes, Marina, we will ride along like this after death,
                    a part of everything except ourselves.
Dark eyes beneath a shaved skull,
you strangle a doll with an old crepe ribbon.

You think of your body swinging from a rope, a hand
holding the other end to squeeze the breath from you.

Though my mother's suicide took years,
her death was precipitous. She spit blood.
An ambulance whine I heard while sleeping two thousand miles away.

What would I have said to her?
My father hit the doctor who told him.

May the doctor stand neck-deep in snow in the after-air
                    for his failing hands.
May he taste the sweetest mincemeat my mother ever baked.
May he never have to speak.
The luxury of our metaphors, the shapes we see & draw

along the edge of anything, may not be the luxury
of our afterlives, the capaciousness

we fear like agoraphobics,

watching the lettering of our names break up like leaf cinders
wafting a few feet namelessly attached to the air,

just one more iridescent feather beginning the day outside
alien as it is, dear latecomer,

dear self, a bit of light from winter's harsh candle.

Hours of the Cardinal

in memory of my mother

With a green patch
of cloth across my forehead,

I feel my mother's hand lifting away,
a fever turned down to an almost imperceptible gas flame.

Mom, you aren't here at all.
I can't lift my hand this high without its falling

the way a day's sun, used up, will drop
out of everywhere into the thick grass in the next yard.

The usual spate of doves descends to the scratch
in the driveway, some with throats the color of a pale rosé.
The cardinal, my favorite, comes at dawn & dusk,

some kind of ancient clock. It's gone,

flying low, sowing a demented whistle in the air,
its undulating trajectory some remarkable evasion of radar.

———————

In the north where the pain was born
water splatters sunlight unevenly across the backs
of her hands so how is she to make sense

of the ghosts that slip over the lip
of her spearmint tea?

For the umpteenth time
she lifts the homemade Christmas card.
On it, four girls in identical dresses
pose for the Politeness Award from the city
                              Boston Post 1935.
She remembers her classmates thought she was pretty
with her "Chinese eyes."

What does the absolute have to do with such
blatant particularity?

She is sitting in her darkened room, like a spider,
skinny legs dragging the air.
She sits in the dark.

She is not here at all.

———————

As the scroll unfurls, I don't know where to place my eyes
among the dissolving brushstrokes, a thousand li per inch.

In the deep grass, the plum tree stands for a day in spring
when a woman walking a thin nervous line along the mountain

miscarries—she doesn't know if it's the child
or herself who is the lost prescience.

She invests each white sepal
with a measure of grief that will not betray her.
She works in shades of damask & vermilion.
Her child

is the black sunflower seed a cardinal pinches in its beak
to wipe on a cold hard branch. The child

is a landscape touched up as we go,
fathomless & full of contour.

Ancient characters: some sinuous lines to say: *mountain,*
others tufted like herons or cranes, all,
in any case, edge the view that mistakenly goes on & on

as do the rivers.

How does the stick bridge—a breath of cinnabar—
cross the chasm between one & another?

———————

The Silk Road, the thread of enterprise,
is also an umbilical cord.

Hour of the Tiger, Hour of the Boar.

A llama lists to one side, jars of love oil
lashed under its belly with cord.

For days, as a child,
I picked the cherries that hang over this road.

They stained my mouth so red
the merchants perched me on the neck of the first horse
to frighten Mongols.

No . . . if I'm there in the past at all
it's as *the imaginary child*

dissolving in & out of a mountain mist
called *God's tears* by the elders & aldermen of the village.

I bathe in the gossipy wisdom of their disappearing years.

In the photograph of a memory
I see myself with the toy soldiers I used to call *uhmas*

screeching from my drooling mouth.

Those real & endless days—too dear to collapse—
are listening to my mother's voice
as it weaves in & out of what I say, her endless

divagations ideal in their single-minded swerve toward home.

———————

We, we could have been anything,
a stark pre-Han tree of bronze
or a stream threading pavilions high in the mountains.

If this body is a house
this gnarled hand is the pear tree in bloom.
The thin white tissues

already conceive of their gentle parachuting to the ground.
Beneath the tree, a woman is weeping.
She rends her silk kimono with a knife.
Small teardrop opals

gird an urn so that her grief contains her son—dead in battle.

He is "the mountain" & "the river," characters
which had to precede, in fact, define those for
"nothingness" or "air."

The last she saw the boy he stood in the mirror.
He flicked a speck of lint from the lapel of his uniform.

A snowflake is burning his cheek.

Beyond a rise in the land
he hears bearded elk churn up the tundra.
He smells the hoof-sparks extinguished in snow.

But his mother is nowhere on the edge of breath,
nowhere at all.

At his feet is a sprig of "Everlasting" crushed by the jealous dead.
They cannot wait to thaw

into many turbulent forms of life.

In the painting, tight buds etched with snow
inch up the black tracery of a branch,
                              like all consolations, failed.
I have no child, or else he stepped into a boat
and pushed off from the muddy shore with a pole
that makes a sucking sound even now as I imagine it.

                    As he lifts his head,
the breeze from the north tells him he's heading away
into whatever life the trees along the shore sustain

which is everything outside the shell he's known
all his life as Father's. . . .

The cardinal reddens the air.

The sun—medallion above the waterways—
could be a sinkhole for a maelstrom of cardinals.

It could be the "nothingness"
where my son spills all his identification cards.

A picture of his mother dissolves in the water
at the bottom of the boat.

On shore, children shriek as they falter
beneath buckets of millet. The business of their song.

The business of the water.

———————

The next time I look out the window
there's a man there with a black shirt stuck to him.
His hand,

the claw of a turkey vulture, closes on a pear.
With a fingernail he nudges a wasp

to a thoroughfare of "wind" that, before now, didn't exist.
Well, sure, the cotton-candy beard

was blowing around on his jaw.

He's talking to a black & white mutt with a red bandanna
tied around its neck.
The old coot, the old mutt, a perfect pair.

Oh, let him talk to the golden windows on the sides of pears.
Oh, let the landscape betray a red splash on the neck of a dog.

It's the redbird deep in the low leaves.

That whistle tells you it's crazy to lie in the woods by yourself
or to sit inside a beehive hut or human skull.

From a great distance it's a lighthouse or the open door
of a kiln where a bodhisattva, in the lotus position, meditates

on a boneless wash of green. It's easy to multiply,
it's easy to fade. That's why dragons

in the shape of clouds
turn their fire on the snow-thick branches of the snowberry.

As my mother began to die, her heart hurt
as though, like a pheasant, it would burst for the sky.

But then no feeling at all.

How does the breath of cinnabar cross the chasm
between one & another?

Stanzas Written at Baba Yaga's

in memory of L. S.

From a live oak, a feeder swings
in a gust of wind I can barely hear
as I reread your postcard of Ayrshires
shiny & staid as showroom cars.

In a Minnesota city clinic
you traced these perfect smoky letters
sung an octave higher than the words
chemo, just three big nasty ones.

We all believed, if anyone,
you'd beat the body's rudeness
the way you strafed each high-jinks
high-school jock with your long best lines.

These always made me want to run home
and write beyond my envy any word
too good for ink. Now there's nothing
to outdo but an ache that grows like algae.

Lynda, did the broken fist of your lung
go limp, your breath quit, the windows silver?
I don't want to remember you
any other way but in that blue

second-hand dress with the low neckline
I always wanted to touch, there, on the breastbone
to know how it felt to tread so lightly,
resilient after years on a Wisconsin dairy

with an army of ash-blond sisters.
You said you loved them because they were there
and you here in the damp gulf plains
where I turn my attention to the wind

as it lifts potato chip bags from the gutter
and filigrees the sheath of rain on the glass.
It's not a clearing of the air exactly,
this watching circumstance bore itself with wind,

but a way to stave off pain:
how red & blue styrofoam balls
inside a metal cage the shape
of the globe burst soundlessly

above a quilt of bingo cards
and your mother's dour stare.
Lynda, I remember a talk we had
after months of my monkish study.

It was cloudy with patches of bright sun
in an umbrella'd café beneath palms.
You lit a Kent & blew the smoke aside
to say, "Oh, Rich, it isn't that bad."

Next to me, rocking in a red chair,
a woman is reading Simone de Beauvoir,
her hair is spiked with a roseate frost.
I kid myself she looks like you

but her glow is artificial,
brightened with the sweet allure
of shaded features that aren't hers
or mine or even yours, Lynda,

in your sweet indifferent palace of thin air.
The window behind her is filling with light
as she hoists a coconut & white rum.
She has her tongue lost in the green meat

of an avocado. She grins a chin-line beard
and brief moustache. She swears
in a language I've never heard,
with words maybe even you would envy.

Summer: Silver Flashing

In the after air is it
pouring rain or bright sun?

It's beyond time, silly one,
crumbling like marl in your hand.

No, what basalt thunderclouds
churn the next gully?

I know the taste of nickel on my tongue,
      conjecture's wafer
marking us with a smudge of ash, an apple of ash on the tongue.

Yes, but will our grandest surmise
pass over an estuary of white candles?

In a mind that is yesterday & landscapeless
I placed a clepsydra of snow—
it thaws one black molasses drop at a time,
      sweet riddance, sweet time.

———————

The sun's fingernail plays pin-the-tail
on this blank sheet of aluminum
curved over the earth,
    the least poetic here & now
among sage & paintbrush: a quonset hut
thrown up after Pearl Harbor at the edge of an airfield.

I can see it in the distance
like a caterpillar contracting beneath the shadow of a hand.

Inside it, across huge tables
atomic scientists rolled blueprints of Jap Basher & Fat Man.

No doubt these men could extirpate every last alien thing,
each bacterium like a sputnik on the breath.
They were good, sweet fathers, stunned
                                    by their goodness,
the way you said the sun stunned you out of everything
after just a walk to the Circle K for bread or milk.

Perched on our postureless couch,
you flushed with the sinister intentions of the sun,
your wrist flopping its lily hand
against a cheek burned the rose of rare quartz.

 Now you're lucky to disappear
into the little we know of you
                              watered down with light
in a state hospital where the dying stuff bills in paper sacks
to expire like albino praying mantises
                              on Etruscan marble.

                    ———————

No doubt these good men
could dismantle your good queer ass for the asking.
But you don't ask.

Your postcards of Big Sur, Palo Alto,
and Port Angeles are a western archipelago
                              petering out to a Pacific rim.
I want you to haunt these lines like a bee in a jar.

But rain begins its quieter, more selfish drumming
against the broken aluminum porch
where I go sometimes to touch the first buds

of the ocotillo, the yucca's blade,
the jumping cholla's concertina wire.

Rusted Christmas angels
whirl from the chameleon limbs
of the paloverde.

Boy, it's really coming down,
silver lances that change direction.

Soon the culverts will spill over the roads,
the *more than enough* pooling in its own,
                              the *Pearl* poet's brides
multiplying like fish roe in the very looking.

Then the tumult will cease
so I can spill out onto gravel juicy as grapefruit,
the rills & gutters driving before them the silt
                              of our determined thought,
which can't hold much of anything too long, least of all *you*.

For sixty ticks of a stopwatch, I'm trying
to think of nothing that is blessed, nothing I can lose.

II

Symmetry

I remember erecting a screened-in porch
for a house I lived in, the staple gun
all afternoon like a giant mosquito

whirring above a sleeper's ear.
One month later, to the day, I found a hummingbird, dead,
and I thought *be careful*

as I turned it over with a long yellow pencil.

It was terrifyingly symmetrical, each wing an inch,
its torso, even its needle nose compass an inch.

Its neck an iridescent emerald.
Its underside a burnt sandalwood ash
coming off a bit with the pencil.

A Half Inch of Blue Sky

Tu Fu, the thick dust of night opens like a melon
                                        cut with an axe.
I have wandered these same blue rivers, blue roads.

I recognize one stone atop another
                        as the Ancients' Arithmetic, the blue surd.
When I reach my friend's house,
his children churn out yards & yards of homemade pasta.

The sweet basil leaves sacrifice themselves
to be washed, to please—they taste like ashes or earth

as, the night we're conceived,
the bodies of our parents taste as they uncouple.

                                I see my father lean over a candle
and cup its flame in his palm: the burnt smell of darkness.

I see my mother wandering in the garden,
her long nightshirt holding the essential shape of the body
                                from which we all withdrew.

———————

My friend sweeps one large rainbow trout
                        through olive oil & breadcrumbs.
Sunny-side eggs stare pop-eyed from the fryer.
At the same time, he threads a blue-eyed fishing lure

with the tiny wires from an old transistor.
His wife recently dead, he's talking
about the blue onion above the dance floor
the night the street women began howling
                              when we asked them how much.
I remember them circling the cone of light
around the pool table.
They clung to us like dust, smoke.
Even the memory of this is smoke

as if they were the perfect characters in a novel,
going off like cherry bombs all at once, on their own.

Tu Fu, when you hear through the thick blue night
two men in the near distance
                              pushing hard on walking sticks,
the *toc, toc* of the sticks pocking marks in the wet dirt,

do you touch the straw ablaze with welcome,
                              three house-post figures,
each cupping a bowl of oily flames?

Or do you blow out the candle
by which you've been reading
and sit in the dark, knees to chin,
listening to the wind in the trees,

the brown moths ticking the bamboo screens
till we pass, till we pass . . . ?

———————

We push the boat from shore
with the sucking sound of mud.

Several black & white buffle-head ducks break from the water.

Then, all is quiet.
In the distance a waterfall, like a rope in thin air,

drops its palaver.

Our tongues, old boats, rot in the coves of our mouths.
Bees breed in the white poppies,
they fill the chalk fissures with sun.
The earth is gentle, the river speeding on.

————————

Behind a Mardi Gras mask of jet-black smoking nostrils
I breathe the ground pepper my friend
tips from a shaker—idly—as if

these beard specks each were time's own pulse
grown still against his porcelain wrist.

Drinking cypress wine till the shops close,
we talk of that day
near White City the dog jumped from the pickup
                    because the dead were whistling
one black octave higher than human hearing.

His wife, dead, so small . . . too white to see,
he remembers a horse that slipped & fell, scaling a cliff.

It broke its neck, he says, in the crotch of a tree.
Diaper was a jet-black gelding.

He says his father let him stop the horse from shrieking.
                              I say *I remember.*

————————

I tell him it's one vast green wash of mountain,
                    a few ochre deer
flinging themselves like arrows across the peaks.

He can't cut a cartographer's crooked line
along the naked constellation of his name.

When the sky opens its floodgates of green water
we can't tell ourselves from the deep smell of sod.

Memory, wet & black, sucks off his shoe.
We make it as far as the bright yellow brushstrokes of bamboo.

We unravel the thin strips of our pallets.

It's the shrine to the Nothing, the unholy word.
We sleep light, like cream coming to the top of coffee.

———————

When a numbnuts, brand-spanking-new Mercedes
runs the light, my friend loses it. He lectures

her steely-eyed coolness inside the air-conditioned car.

He imagines his two boys like astronauts, for a second, flying
till the seatbelts catch them

and the fender-bender completes its ten-second tit-for-tat.
No one will blame the sun smelting us from over the palms.

He tells me "These are my two boys" as if, in his mind,
they were twins banking from side to side

inside the amniotic sack: *it's bright out there*
calls a thin electric wire of a voice

over the singe of air: *it's bright out there.*

———————

As he is dropping cornflowers
on his wife's casket,

blue veins at his temples,
he's looking back through the sound of deerflies,

the song of the reeds & the loosestrife.

A man with reel & leaky boots
is wading deeper into the water.
On the tip of a cattail a redwing blackbird

flashes its epaulet, the spirit of the smoking mirror.

He's wondering how the distinct marks of the past
can throb with incandescence as if with new meanings

they would burst aflame. He thinks he should have

done something different, loved her somehow different
so that when the time comes to give up his body

lifting through the open mouth of the dead like ghostly laundry,
a voice doesn't say, no, we don't want you now, no.

You must rock your wife on the hard blue nail of your life.

———————

On the mesa,
the sound of deer hooves on asphalt
lifts them out of themselves,
                          invisible & giant.
After years, he could only feel this
with his young waitress
                  on the sly
as if it were the secret of himself
held from himself inside.

He'd tell his wife
we practiced till after midnight
at my uncle's body shop,
                  the shop of the body,
a lie repeated so seamlessly it enclosed us:

a steel chassis laid open
                    like a cadaver,
blues riffs redoubling in shiny fenders.

One day, at their house, she took my right palm
and ran her fingernail down the vein
as if it were a coastline

along the too white ocean of what we give away.
"Your thumbnail's grown thick," she said,
watching the kids' baseball sweats

twirl in the dryer.

But now she's gone.

A firefly ceases its signal
as he unwinds the hose

to spray a mist over his miniature pear trees.
There's no quieter love than theirs,

the *woman* & *man* exactly ten feet apart.
He paces it off,

his cherry high-tops heel to toe, heel to toe,
till he's measured the distance

love's pollen flies.

The two boys run the hall, crying,
                    the smell of talc
and the burnt sandalwood underside of dreams.

Monsoons sluice the roof,
a monotonous crescendo of water & sound.

I click on the nightlamp,
the shape of a blue chubby airplane
                    fathering its small aureole
the way, last month, one of his headlights
up-canted from a ditch of fireweed
must have spent its measly light
                    on a black motherless sky
as he sobbed, an egg brown bruise on his temple.

From a text I can barely read
I begin copying a reprimand against suicides:
for eternity they will be ghosts crammed in the eaves
or drifting on the waters—that's what it says.

But maybe
it's not a question of will
since we're all headed, flying or erratically floating
toward Ch'ang-an

where firewood is the price of cinnamon, rice the price of pearls.

———————

All this rain is the mothers.

Jags of light across the sky.
No longer the shaved shafts of oak,
this is all that's left of them,

watery ghosts in the creases of clouds.

They've had their fill of this,
they just want to fall all over everything,
                    toss a glass feeder

through the last nostalgic whiff of pipe smoke, wisteria
and, from the kitchen, the crushed cloves of garlic.
Then a thunderclap. That's the mothers too,
getting the final word in.

Dad's pointing to the pages of birds:
here's the scarlet ibis, the kingfisher, too many birds.
"Mommy isn't mad, it's Darth Vader's ship
taking a direct hit from the Millennium Falcon."

The boys' cry is winding down
                              like an air raid siren
into no sound before the sound is gone.

———————

*Tu Fu, you roll out our shiny pallets
among the fiery dragon clouds. In the mountain fog*

*two boys daub the carapace of a lumbering tortoise
with blue paint. The invisible birds whistle*

*from the yellow strokes of bamboo, they whistle
and then are gone. My friend lists to one side,*

*spilling amber liquid over his teeth.
Master, what good is it*

*if I won't be able to step inside his death mask, cold & damp.
I will even be peripheral to the events*

the family priest will summarize as his life.

*I might convince myself that this is best, the only light
by which we at least see our destinies veering drunkenly
                              toward us at top speeds.
Coach was always pleased when the pass slipped*

from the corner of the eye
to hit the breaking forward on the run for the layup or the dunk
so if my death is not his, dear master, tell me
will his at least lead me on?

———————

The morning his wife's body
lay among the blond bones of Tinker Toys,
popcorn scattered everywhere like a fine net of alyssum,
it wasn't odd or ordinary,

this body domestic, cold, blue, beyond us.
He held her for all the good he couldn't do,

the openly sexual spray of light across everything,
the honeylocust ringed with mist & rising
the way a cinnamon stick rises from a mug of tea,
                                              sweet & numinous.
This must be how she felt, the pleasant waves of lethargy
dizzying the yard to the river

as if, through a rare translucent gem,
she were looking at the river of the heart.

It must have hurt like hell, that love.

———————

After the funeral
the younger boy reveals a wedge of tangerine,
                          a toy orange sloop on his palm.
He says take me out in the boat,
teach me to draw up the bright rainbow fish.

But beneath the azure disk of the sun
someone is rowing the boat at the edge of sunlight
and the glare of blue. I tell him we must

be happy with the wind's hand waving goodbye,
                                someone's fingertips
touching each of our features—ghostly masseuse.

Across beach braille, his sneakers squeak
"dad-boy, dad-boy." Behind us,

the unholy light of imminences,
honeylocust & morning moon.

Dear master,
I can't lose you any farther
than the delicate wooden bridges
connecting mountain village to distant peak—

that colossal birthday gift, one thin intermittent
strip of ribbon—
ten li, a thousand li: we can't measure it.

This is my elegy to water.
This is my book of the dead.

We're stuck in our words, Tu Fu,
like a sea turtle drowning in a dory's net.
Ensnared,

the blue shape our breath swerves is all
that will not be made tractable.
It is human, enough,

empty as the sea.
Why am I going on like this?

No longer even the airy nest of the body,
you can't alight, not even a toehold.

And you can't fly: ovoid blue, sky blue.
I don't know how these two boys feel
without their mother, one numb river

of feeling. A thousand glacial peaks
would draw our eyesight up past the pavilions
and farther up, endlessly into the clouds

if not for the few bold, almost child-like strokes
heavy with snow
from which the alabaster faces of snow monkeys
stare back at us.

The Black Venus:
For Max Ernst

1.

Max, I lean a photo of Josephine Baker
in this box lined with black construction paper,

it looks like a miniature dollhouse
lined with morose wallpaper that would caution
even the young Mark Rothko.
But, as in his work,
we must distinguish the shapes of panthers
in the black expanse—her emblem—

as she poses in Miss Bricktop's new *boîte de nuit*,
her hair oiled flat against her skull like a Black Venus.

Maybe you saw her dance—all lips & hips—
her skin one shade darker than honey
turning in the hot lights the ghostly shade
of Lalique glass. I imagine you two
passing in the street, her entourage parting for her
behind the leash her leopard Chiquita draws
as the crowd leans from the cat
and back again toward her.

Fifteen years her senior,
you will die within months of her—

that year I chucked my job counting numbers
to follow your ghost through the sandstone
of Sedona, Arizona, with a blank book for poems.

Didn't we emerge from the same prehistoric egg
amid sparks of jet & obsidian embedded in the hills
of Montmartre? "Only Negroes can excite Paris."
Fernand Léger said to Daven, who marveled

at black women dancing the quai of Gare St.-Lazare,
their *feu d'artifice* under sooty gray glass.

2.

One night upstairs in her room at the theater
off the Champs-Elysées,
watching the letters *Citroën* flash the Eiffel Tower
with the sensational new effect called Néon

she whispers it's a new age, baby, damn straight.

And the next night
as she weaves with "the speed of a hummingbird"
through the tree-trunk legs of the giant Joe Alex,
you can't keep your eyes off her.
Later, schnitzel burning on an illegal hot plate
in your room above the Pantheon,
you begin your first paragon Afrique
born from a pair of lovebirds, a pink macaw.

In my photograph of her,
she's playfully staring down the replica of an elephant,
already imagining her failure
in your country & hers,

her girdle of phallic bananas turned to the tusks
poachers hack from elephants.

3.

Does what is dark & magnificent
require we hack it,
the way the words of the American tourist
in the fashionable restaurant

hacked a silence: *Back home, a nigger woman belongs in the kitchen.*
In my mind, as in a movie, you stride out of the dark
like a Hollywood hero & bash the man on his ear bone,
the blood like a snail trail on his collar.

Years later, during the occupation,
my movie's still running:

your small round head buried in her breast
as the car swerves south. She's telling you
how every night she dreams about her half-sister
Willie Mae peering in between the blinds
at the late-night doctor's office
above a drugstore in St. Louis

where the girl bled to death from a botched abortion.

She tells you how the Hotel St. Moritz hailed her
by asking she give the lobby a wide berth
and use the service elevator,

all the while your heart about to explode with love & fear
as you pass another checkpoint,
the contraband petrol in champagne bottles
in the trunk of the car.

4.

Ah, to explode
with Josephine in the final number of *très sauvage*
in an egg-shaped gold cage of fire,

to transcend the world she saw as the horror of men
returning home from war with only one arm, one leg, one eye. . . .

Today I read that the cop who bludgeoned Rodney King
over fifty times will get a reduced sentence.

I imagine this man bent over a slab of meat
as the black brothers in the maximum security
lean against the walls, stretching their Achilles' & gesticulating.

But just as surely as she had to leave again her country
these cops will serve a few months in a condo.
One of Gauguin's dark maidens,

she will climb the stairs, much older now,
radishes from the garden trailing from her hands.
With their fronds she'll tickle awake her adopted children
in the many bedrooms of the house in the Dordogne.

She is the pure black shape of a panther
undiscovered in Lascaux.

In my box, this *boîte de nuit,*
I've juxtaposed her image with an over-exposed picture
of a black cat. Eight different edges of the same cat
stare straight ahead, as if on stage

but the ninth stares off across her dark skin
to a box with slats I've turned on its side
to stand for a jail made of blond pine.

Inside is a demonic clown-head on a spring:
a jack-in-the-box the size of a swollen thumb.

I call this "Homey the clown incarcerated
for wearing whiteface, August 1993" after a popular

black television figure,
not Step'n Fetch It, Hannibal above the ruins of Rome.

III

Blackout

A. L. 1925–1987

With the fidelity of sand
                pouring from hand to pudgy hand,
the light still picks out the curve of your cheek
and my hand, trembling, still reaches to massage,
with lotion, the welts rising on your hip,
a terrain I can't pretend to maneuver
                with any degree of accuracy.
Is it something like where you are now, mother,
swelling with all the moments of our lives?

You left, on my buttocks, the mark of your hand
when I wouldn't unbunch myself from bedclothes
                to sing at morning Mass.
Now every single day is Sunday, each wound
as vacant as the peal of bells.

Oh, poor pure Agnes, too numb to sin—
one lost spring, in your johnny
you wanted me to touch your broken body,
you, who had taught me so well to live outside my own.

I remember the wrists, years later, crossed in your lap—
the absolute zero of embalmer's blood.

You didn't remember falling, backwards, down the stairs.
You fell back through years, effacing enough

of the pain that I didn't even exist.

Archaic Smile

Skin pallid, lips painted,
jars of pills on the bedside,
you are beautiful.

In bed, your spine like an electric cable
knocked down in a storm, you are beautiful.

Wearing a plaster corset with a sickle of roses
curved beneath a breast, you are beautiful.

Each of the fingers
on your left hand
is also braced—huge rings. Two on the thumb,
and on the finger after all these years
still the fuck-you finger

is a ring with delicate demarcations
of longitude & latitude,
a replica of your beloved hemisphere
reduced to half a hard-boiled egg
on the raft of your bed.

It's 1951,
the day I strangled out my first cry.
It was for you, Frida, it's for you.

Holding a life-sized sugar skull with your name
written in white worms of icing across a chocolate hairline,

with white loops of infinity streaming back over the pate,
you turn to me

and I tip my hat, saying a lot of nothing,
saying, "You are beautiful, Frida, simply beautiful!"

You peel one of the eyebrows off the death's-head
and lift it toward me.

"It's cinnamon, silly, eat it."

With Arapaho Dreamcatcher

Caught on strings leached with the glue
of horses too old to race, sire, or even die,
                                    the good ones
held in the mandibles of the dead-eye *arachnid*

shoot through the loops of sweet grass
into a few brightly colored tail feathers
tilting in the cross drafts.

From my noisy pets, I've added the dried tubular
blood feathers of the budgerigar & the cockatiel
in hopes the dreams will be sweet & familiar.

In one dream you're holding up sheets of hamburger,
the letters of your poems printed roseate
against the darker red meat of the page.

When I telephone, you are kind not to say
this is obviously a dream of jealousy
                        which is what I would say,
eager to be merciless to myself.

But the dream remembers you standing ankle-deep
on the killing floor at the slaughter house in Oklahoma.

It remembers you & me standing in a field of scattered weeds,
off in the distance a billboard offering one black scrap of shade.

You're bent over a terminal with a screen
that, in the irrefutable logic of dreams,
configures the answers of time & space & circumstance

that will allow us inside these original desert nothingnesses
where dark automobiles collide with their dreams.

For us, white stretchers borne by ghosts
float into sight, the not-so-silent lacerations of the dying.

One girl's rachis pokes through her lower back
like the bare pole of a tree, her face sprayed red with glass.

A man with his head half shaved is walking in circles,
his eyes closed, repeating just above his breath

these lines from Scriptures, "For when we were yet
without strength, in due time Christ died for the ungodly"

and I wonder if, with the ungodly arrogance
of the fundamental, he accuses these here, dying on our hands,

or if he comforts them
                    in the more modest millennial sense
of what the dream is saying about the girl
clutching her French horn:
the mouthpiece missing, the cornucopia crimped.

She wants to play the dream of mercy
inaccessible as mercy's pain, as impossible as the distant back
of a billboard beneath the sun.

Its rusted cross-struts & scaffold
offer a solace but not for anyone we could name.

Two Deaths in
San Bernardino

The enemies of the spirit
                want to destroy the body,
the stink of cooling flesh a benevolence for the flies,

their multifaceted eyes a golden green fire of apperception.

The cruiser's beacon closes its milk-white eye,
no motive to alibi—a body
with the longest paper cut in history
opens like an envelope in the grassy envelope of a ditch.

The syringa fill the air with orange scent,
the remaining few silent kids too tired to lift their batons
and click out their names on the picket fence.

Now from the Zen Center the monks
all in a row & in silence carry buckets of water
                              sloshing as they go
across the blond plank of hacked sequoia
through the fine combed hair of gray gravel.

Inside the fatigue of their labor
they rock sacks of mulch over the roots of a young oleander
thinking of wide red blossoms, a bright red wine
poured slowly onto rice paper. For a few minutes

a dog turd is an Eastern temple, turrets twisted to the sun.
The flies are celebrating their windfall,
                    tomorrow's perfectly manicured lawn
beneath the sun's brash flakes & the delirious daffodils.

Inside, the master is dying,
his roan-colored cowering heart kicking his ribs.

Features a shade darker than the dome of flesh
hardened over the skull, he's stripping the finger leaves
of the lupine & beating his chest with them.

Soon he will be a blossom of flame,
the rose petals curling black as dung beetles in the fire.

Some wish to strip away every last thing—

we don't know if the song of the deceased is a dewdrop
crashing over the falls to join the waves

or if it's a grievous red ember in the heart.

Like Glass Pyramids
at Midnight

This is November—
laid out on the dining room table,
my uncle, dead,
            waiting to arise, his arms out a bit
like the wings a caged bird lifts to cool itself.

He's waiting for a hand
to run a washcloth over him.
Outside, dead rain stipples the matted grass.

Maybe they will wait on our ablutions, being dead,
since this *being* is nothing if not solicitous:
a waiter with a linen squared over his forearm,
asking "Is everything all right?"

as we balance ourselves
above the blackened redfish seasoned with curry
and sop up the sauce

with our daily bread.

———

Our seasons, like our ceremonies,
sweeten us. Elm leaves

press against the fence, like Haitian refugees
not wanting to go home.

The Earthmans, my father's friends,
plant a tree for each new deceased.
In the spring a Pacific madrone

will butter its popcorn buds
against dull green leaves
and a warm breeze will finger the fretwork
of our living thoughts.

But, for now, the sapling in its black foil
constricts its roots inside my hands.

Jog & Jacob are twins
of the patient dead, their name

chosen by a man who existed before names
in a soft country for charred bones,
                    Friends of the Earth, singed free of it.

That day in early June,
the piss smell, the sun bright,
his palm unfurled two dice he'd saved
from crap games on Midway.

His battalion,
like trees through a shredder, he said, all mulch.

When my Aunt Lily hurls the yellow clay
of her cardigan into his grave,
even looking at the sky seems obscene

as it presses down on our Model Homes & vain little trees
like a man pressing his weight

against the scarred glass of the peep show—
the woman, inside, all green,

the holograph of a bee
caught in its own paraffin.

––––––––––

The cat mummy stares down
the pots & pans of culture
just as the cat hunts the Nile
                    for newts & smoking minnows.
As I stare through the glass
at the man black as bitumen
I think of the sea horses, rude as the air's kiss.

I see their regal heads tipping forward
as if conferring upon a matter of state.

The man, of some means, orders
his body sweetened with white honey.

Now, his one last big toe
points to the north, a mushroom
sprouting from his linen-wound left foot.

Through the nose, the high priests
draw his brain out
                    with an iron hook & then
with a sharp Ethiopian stone
incise the abdomen,
                    a small red tight-lipped smile
to inject, through a waxed reed, the oil of cedar—
the body an ancient fiery cocktail.

––––––––––

My fingertips on the sweaty glass,
the capillaries ignite whatever it is

they reach toward, even this armada
of miniature stallions.
Being alive, they move in imminent space, a hush
just vacated, like a shout at midnight
followed by a bottle crashing on a wall
and then nothing, the all-surrounding nothing
like the octopi flowerets
on my uncle's hospital window,
raindrops like glass pyramids on the glass.

———————

This is November
disencumbering, dead leaves scraping the drive,
the grid of brown vines
climbing the side of the house.

My aunt is preserving his absence,
we enter,
the dust motes already thickening
in the sweet scent of English Leather
she palms on the swinging mirror.
On the bureau stands a picture of them
with Bob Cousy in a school gym
in Worcester, Massachusetts,
the letters of a banner moving past the frame of the picture.

She flicks a Mantle, even a Clemente in the mirror's crease
inside which we could see
if she tilted the glass
a hospital-tucked, chestnut-brown army blanket
white with cat hair: the spartan

marriage bed.

———————

O, the sweet insipid innocent
leaning off the dock in a brilliant dying light.

O, his blinking eyes of milk.

He tips his giant toy sail to the left
                    one child's nautical inch
where it belongs, beyond his freckled touch.

His name is John, a boy's name
meaning *the water is gracious,* meaning it takes everything away.

In Defense of the Body

Though there's no record
of the conferring of a degree
Henry Vaughan practiced medicine at Newton
on the river Usk all those years
            with a fair local reputation.
No doubt he had his share stretch dead on the table,
as close at hand & as far away
as the meal the widow, out of habit,

leaves out on the other side of the candle.
Nobody, not even the saint of a wife,

wants to hear about the little alien stars
on the vertebrae, the ankle
pivoted backwards, its hairline crack,
the days on crutches making each block an odyssey.

At the Cloisters above the Hudson,
the crutches clacking on the stairs like salmon,
I try to rest, but the ghost in a blazer
            asks me to move on
past the last wall of tapestry where the huntsmen
pierce the white hide of the unicorn.

I swing my body in rhythm to the crutches
all the way to the Natural History Museum
to see Lucy, the first woman, Eve & Lilith's
simian triplet an array of bones on soft cloth.

Okay, Henry, so your argument is foolproof,
the body is a cesspool, a sulphur-spewing vestige
                                        of the golden soul
that reigned somewhere back in unrecognizable time.

But let me tell you
we carry our own deaths inside us,
                                intricate glass telephone booths
from which we hear the incessant ringing
piercing the eardrum with a black winter branch.

These days my stomach rejects every morsel,
passing gas from above & below
                            to quote the Pakistani M.D.
who seems to blush behind his beautiful dark skin.

On the screen in the x-ray room, the cloudy mass
of my stomach looks like a bota bag I got as a souvenir
                                at a bullfight in Monterrey,
my large & small intestines filibustering
like proud scandalous politicians.

This is my cry to the dying carcass
to let the hunters hurl me into a bottomless pit.
This is Vaughan's argument, I guess, for the universal.

For Dianne
Wherever She May Be

Not far from here our immigrant parents
worship the gray texture of food from the sea.
They christen a fishing fleet, a blast
                      of frantic white doves
breaking from the hold of a ship.
On deck, Theresa—our parish saint—
still trying to dance beyond herself,

looks boozy & self-involved. The last I knew,
you lived with your husband in a small town home in Columbus.
If my bet is right we won't ever reach each other

or suffer much. It was the summer

we danced with flashlights into the damp hell of the cedar swamp,
singing *Ding Dong, The Witch Is Dead.*

Nixon had finally come clean,
his noodle of a face on every channel,
contrite & sallow as a jaundiced pup.

No doubt, your politics have shifted, like most's,
toward some crystalline future
that even our children can't see
                  as if they expected us

to erect over them immutable domes of snow,
white cinders rising & falling in our wrists.

I think of the night all of us from the college,
                              in couples & alone,
on the cold boards extending out into the sea,
rehearsed our fears, singing over the water.

We bellowed, like seals, *tequila, first & ten, love-me-do.*

Later, we dozed & woke & talked again.
We couldn't tell when we finally fell asleep. Just then,

a sleeping bag came alive with the humping of I guessed
two bodies, awkward swaying at first then a faster

more rhythmic thudding—
I was sure I was dreaming someone's murder.

After a while they turned from each other,
their bodies like dunes against the moon & sea.
But what these two were to each other I couldn't say

unless it were as the moon is to the sea, an intimate distance.
For a moment the waves
splashing against the wharves were a tender sort of lovemaking,
tiny seismic sighs of *yes, yes.* . . .

In the quiet, I remember imagining the sigh
of sea foam, like lace, on the seawall.
I remember listening

to the tiny explosions of alcohol in the blood
as though, through some wholly personal demolition,
we might destroy, from the inside out,

the pale patina of the world: one giant
pink-skinned mannequin smacking the windshield
of a car: no stuffing, nothing.

We wanted to burn most everything that was our parents.

What I remember about that summer
is not so much the huddling of a generation
that thought to love itself, but the cold run
of the bay that, like a chocolate Persian,

bounds effortlessly in, then curls up
to lick itself clean. Dianne, that night
you must have shimmied over cool chaste sheets
to make room for me

sleepwalking back from the dangerous edge of things.
I think I remember a T-shirt ripped at the shoulder.

In the morning, a little firm in the briefs,
I turned from you.
And then the whole house was alive—

the birds in first light filling the windows,
the docks, the trawlers,

even the fishing nets,
as if all of this would go up in flames
against black water.

Some Weeks before an Autumn Wedding

1.

The mystic Welsh doctor Henry Vaughan saw us
                            as blown milkweed pods & dust
billowing up from beneath our wheels
till it settles back on the shine of windshield
and what we've become stares through what we've been,
                            dust to dust, a comfort to us
who keep looking down at these hands waiting to stretch
a *Kyrie eleison* across the mute tusks of dead animals,

waiting to douse with kerosene the thin walls of honeycomb,
striking a match to the sound that is a hole in space.

                    Through low branches
the car shushes, elderberries smeared on the glass.

We push our bodies up a hill topped by a black oak,
                            no hooded figures awaiting us,
just the scythe of the spine curving forward
until our bare foreheads kiss bare earth.

2.

The black branches' infinite indecision
crisscrosses the twilight.

Two men, brothers, we share a past we can't reconstruct.

All we've got is this derailed locomotion
of speech to go on inventing stories of the dead.
I can't recall one single event
                    from my first six years.
Tall glasses of Irish whiskey, Catholicism's curse,
these alien heredities erase who a child is,
                    nameless, perfect, & extinct.
In the distance fir trees blacken themselves
                    into what isn't behind them.
Licorice-thick as old coffee,
the wind goes on with its meticulous revision,

the illegible marginalia of nightshadows,
the living ghosts we are.

3.

Near dawn we stir a stick in the branches,
an etiquette the snake recognizes,
                    evacuating its palace.
Our bodies blunder where there isn't a path—
coronas of pulsing berries dropping beneath blades of light.

The first clots tick the bottom of the pail.
The rest of the gathering is fastidious berry
on top of berry silent as frogspawn.

Some taste like dew-drenched gossamer
hung on the light, some taste like smoke.

Henry Vaughan's body is dust, it must, by now, by heart,
know that the tie of bodies doesn't last,
each berry quickly plucked
until the branch is skeletal,
                no love or memory
to languish here, except on the tongue & then not even there.

No doubt Lazarus is the Bible's Houdini
eventually drowning in the glass case of all he's dreaming.

These are not imaginary flights wide of a faithful grave.
These are the accurate black flecks of nectar.

4.

A gray drone, proletariat bee,
drums the glass in the den.

You stand in the doorway, its wings pinched back,
like a sliver from a honeymoon mirror,
                one thousandth of all the ill luck
multiplied in the little terrors of light
a chandelier casts when the breeze from a window
revises a thousand crystals.

You slip from your wallet a photograph of your fiancée,
                cupping it in your hand,
the laminated surface of her cheek warm from your body.

The hum of bees is everywhere in the clover,
the sound so dangerously soothing
we take it for the coursing of the blood,
                the *Expect Nothing*
Buddhists hum somewhere in the back of the throat,
hoping it brims over their lips
with the awesome being that is released

when we snatch an elderberry from a low thicket
and crush it in the teeth.

5.

The one flesh come together with one flesh,
that moment when the body radiates beyond itself,
like a gas lantern, when she imagines herself extinct.

Father rises above her, eyes rolled back.
Later, morning-sick, hanging clothes, she watches a slip
blow from sight & so bent on fetching it,

wanders dawn streets in a town she doesn't know,
listening to birds go on about how bright the light is
as if hands had picked over the white sale of her mind.

In the neon foyer of a diner called Ken's
the simplified sound of her footfalls
tells her she must end every last thing she's been.

A cigarette blackens the napkin's delicate monogram
letter by letter as she gobbles America's meal of the dead—
meat burned in a circle, blond fries curled at the end.

6.

Maybe it's a country called Perfection,
                    Mom's notion
of the Absolute with the charm of local color—
the sun unnaturally blue in her above-ground swimming pool,
                    so much splashed water.
She used to sun herself on a float
                    with an armrest for a drink,
no more errands, all of us off somewhere.
But the placid look on her face was the one drink

we saw all through childhood, a fountain spring.
Weren't we her perfect priest, her most valuable player?

She worried that you'd never be serious
                    while I, pathologically so,
knew you could sell anything & so could sell yourself.

Now you drive between New York & Boston, New York & Philly,
even talk over the phone with a broker in Maryland
                    who speaks so slowly you're not sure
you even want the spare part you've doodled on the pad,
waiting for him to make his sentence whole.

Now, you're getting married, a whole new sense of wholeness,
                    The Sun & The Moon in one sky,
an understanding between the sexes,
which is this Earth—children like shuttlecocks

between the milk of burning daylight
and the obsidian of lustrous night.

7.

Really it's the selling, what our mother
quoting her mother called *the gift of the gab,*
                    that makes us theirs,
how we shared the umbilical cord like elves playing tug-of-war,
twins married to the word—ink & noise.

Without kids, you say, we're just red trail markers
in a forest no one visits, scarlet ascots
looped on the silver backsides of leaves.

When we were children in the woods behind the cemetery
where adventure began, we came upon a thicket & plundered it,
an artery of elderberries against my wrist.

White was the color of the laminated bodies
                         we smutched with our fingers,
nudie pages like rattled doves against the leaves.
We sang *worms crawl in, worms crawl out*
to sneer at ceremony, but it was the mess
                         that made us squeamish,
a child's notion of the body as clean hard work,
not beauty's juices, not beauty's dust.

                    8.

We unfold the dark wings of the Ouija
to ask what names the dead give the unborn.

But through the hysterical planchette
a woman named Eunice Plummer
wants us to stop her brother Stan
                         from boarding United Flight 131,
leaving Detroit at 11:10.

As we stare out to where the black oak
is barely visible in battered moonlight,
we wonder why the dead would beseech a loved one
                         to keep his distance
unless the after air is nothing like we imagine,
a toxic haze of unsatisfied dream bodies
crammed in a room, unable to lift their wings.

Perhaps in punishment for letting them die, we write
our names in foot-high letters across the nightdew
                         until our arms thicken & cramp
as in grade school when the teacher made us
fill a blackboard with Palmer Method's hoops & swirls.

9.

As boys, we shimmied a praying mantis
into a neighbor kid's toy oven,
                    then flipped the switch,
the very idea of supplication razed to cinders.

As boys, we began each Lent
with a priest's thumb ash between the eyes.

One Easter she fell behind the dryer,
the rumble of clothes burning her cheek,
the amber hue of whiskey turned the anemic
clear-eyed punch of vodka.

Of course by then I was elsewhere—
anywhere but home in my inky blood.
Hers, when I arrived at the wake, was the zero
                        of embalmer's fluid.
I kept waiting for her to speak
but, for once, the word I had was final.

So this is the afterlife: words spoken to the air,
a vocation: the rosary with an Irish cross
entangled in the fingers,

a mother's-ring spilling its rainbow of birthstones
out of her small white hands.

10.

Snapping briars, two cardinals
spill up into the light from their thick low nest.

We must be frightening to the pure red breath of song.

Male & female, they crisscross the branches,
        like huge sparks that don't catch.
I keep them in sight as long as I can.

When the blood crisscrossing the back of her knee
grew still in her veins, the doctors had to amputate.

Afterwards, she wanted me to draw the curtain
against a gorgeous May morning.

Two cardinals, male & female,
weaved through the freshly planted young trees
outside the hospital.

Would I be lying if I said I watched
through the tissue of the curtains their incendiary mime?
And will she hold it against us

if, tonight, above the dark rise of the levee,
in search of those dying falls of music,
like everyone else running from the terror inside love's voice,

we uncover her whole beaten self everywhere in the sky?
I tell you, brother, the universe is a bitter surprise for desire,
born at such a distance from the mother,

the north star emerging from night clouds. . . .

11.

The dead's children must, by now,
        have a sense of themselves,
what with all this fierce inattention,

the kind that burns a bare shoulder through impossible haze,
the way the discipline of words will turn
to the late autumn bursts of seed—winter furrow, white ice.

We make ourselves perfect with each loss.

In all this cloverleaf burnished with the sun
                            & the sound of bees,
your body backlit by fire makes mine
all consciousness, black & solid as the oak trunk,
its bark splitting apart as if stalled halfway between itself
and some miraculous metamorphosis.

12.

Inside the urn of the body is our facsimile,
                            our ghostbody,
that part of us that hovers close to bliss
      the way egret eggs in sparse brush sit above water,
but after waiting without malice
all these years of humiliation and busted hope,
all these shaky years of moving forward

how will we know we *are* bliss if we can't even sniff
the old-man's beard & lamb's ears
                with their mint scent,
the pollen's dust thumbed into oblivion's blue olfactory mirage.

The dogwood blow beneath the caress of an invisible hand.

I say the dead are out of doors,
they catholicize whatever surface we set our eyes on,
a night sky awash with unindividuated stars.

In the white heat of the ritual pyre,
a berry's pinpoint of blood
crystallizes before it novas into nothing

where even envy can't grow.

13.

Though he wonders why
my wife stands all the way up on her own
without the burning lampposts of Security & Children,
what I like about my brother is
                he senses that the vocabulary
of cloverleaf & bee sting is supposed to be beyond us
so that we can wander inside it,
                            safe from knowing too much.
After swinging the censer all through Easter Mass,
we watched the priest draw the alb's embroidered linen
over his head, standing bare to the waist,
his skin creased with sweat,
                   a silence that resurrects itself
as we descend into the thicket,
the sun in blots behind us as if radiating from the earth,
the flowerets everywhere in gold filigree,

a white porcelain monstrance laid down on its face.

14.

Tempted to bring sons & daughters into this world,
St. Francis whipped his "Brother ass"
                   for this is what he called his body.
Thomas of Celano tells that even this
didn't kill the desire

so he cast his naked body in a pile of snow,
gathered handfuls in the moonlight,
seven lumps like human figures: one wife,
two sons, two daughters, one manservant, one maid,
                           all dying of cold.
I'm not sure if this drove the unchaste longings
from his breast. All I know is
we cut with a Swiss army knife the heart of the black oak
and bury my mother's miniature Irish cross.

Later, sterilizing empty jars,
our wrists & hands red as brick from the water,
we cut the cheesecloth into strips
to strain the nasty tang of elders
                    into a heady young swill
to toast our mother who is dead & will never come back,

to toast your betrothed, the bodies of a man & a woman
light as chalcedony & as strong.

The Corpse Washing

What is this shame we feel for her, being dead,

as she lies there, her flesh cooling, on a table,
what blush easing the furniture of her body
toward the invisibility in a mirror

where no shadow is turning, nothing, not even a wasp
burrowing an exact inkspot in the curve of a pear?
This is the way Augustine says that it is

with God, when the breath stops—no red poppies
bobbing senselessly through their shadows
like mutineers. In one impossibility

my mother & I are sitting on cool blue shale above the Pacific,
watching a few men kiss basketballs off a backboard.

Flushed with sun & adrenaline, their damp bodies dry in the wind.
They drive, pull up & shoot. We hoot & clap,
the smack of shale on shale all the way down into the sea.

In an Instant

IN MEMORY OF LYNDA

White with the mortician's art, her face
still manages to sneer at us, a rhubarb stain

floating beneath the skin like a predatory fish.
This troubles us, doesn't it, insists we unforgive

our own calm breath, the way, in a small theater
before he reads, Mandelstam watches two men in overcoats

ask two women in the front if they will please move?
"We must have these," he imagines them saying,

as if these chairs were the baker's last desserts
delicately drizzled with a thin white string of frost

like the zebra markings of the finch he saw one twilight
through a window in Moscow. Isn't everyone frightened

that, when the time comes, two fingers at the lover's throat
won't be intimate enough? One of the men lifts his pant

to scratch beneath a thin clean sock. In the instant
the women take to comply, the poet rearranges his poems

so, right from the top, there will be reasons for taking notes,
but, from this easy distance, what the great man looks like,

head thrown back, eyes closed, his words like time itself
hovering there between us, is all that matters. We know the rest:

the men take down each word the poet utters, & two days later,
he disappears like the bright quick blossom of the cyclamen,

all the poses it can flash through in an instant—
bared skull to operatic whiteface—our one visage.

To My Deceased Mother

1.

Just as the caver rappels the sheer drop,
the beam of his flashlight sucked black,

I can't retract the face I first turned toward your voice.
The bones the breath of my cheeks aren't even mine.

These days I shear every pleasure from the igneous,
uncover the one shape, the one boy . . .

the original infant death mask
cooled now to Janus split between the new year & the last.

Words escape the muck of what is the desire to mouth them
by betraying feelings that refuse themselves to rock.

2.

One night we dig up your body, alone
these six years, & draw a blade down
between the breasts & pry open the ribs.

Inside, we place an ivory music box,
some tune that seems it must be spiritual
like ice melting among opal & obsidian

or like some imperfect vertebrae of pearls
the roots of the damask will clasp & devour.
Waving aside, with my left hand,

the dust that was your flesh,
I cup a living song sparrow in my right, & lay it
frightened, next to what's left of your heart.

Then I add a rosary, the dry hardened paste
of rose petals. But no looking glass
garish enough for Antoinette or Josephine,

Catherine of Russia or the Queen of the Nile,
could forgive us now as it drops, despite itself,
through the dark void of your bowels.

3.

If I plumb the last pith & marrow
of your invisible body
will I taste the bludgeoning vapor of the days
when, humming snatches of song,

you slid the rocking-stick against my cradle
the way the blowers on Murano fill the glowing shape of a bird,
their lips a ten-foot tube from what they breathe?

If you would believe this,
that I would let you molder in the damp earth,
leave you finally, completely, on your own,

if you would believe this, the buzzard drifting the thermals,
dropping through what remains of you in this world,

then maybe I could live with the abstraction of the great dead.

4.

Just beyond the road I watch the snow sift down
the way the powdered sugar would when I was young
shaking it on gingerbread cut in the shape of hands.

I remember hands like these, creamy plastic hands
pointed in prayer, hung on a nail over a disheveled bed.
I can't look at your face, years later, dead,

the scorch of ice behind the skin, the veins at your temple,
blue. Does the undertaker have to snap the arthritis
in your fingers to release the mother's-rings,

their rainbows? In this memory I feel as helpless as you
lifting your invisible hand close to my chin,
the black stitch of my beard like typeface. I back away,

a ghost in a ghost of snow powdering this meadow
in homage to all of you dancing in homage to yourselves,
your skin milk-white & hard on the eyes in all this

falling crystal fired by the light from the moon.
Wouldn't it be sweet to dance in step with you,
bodies & minds shorn of everything but the eternities

blown through them—the breath of horses, white smoke,
snow beneath giant hooves, cold hushed hollows of air
kicked up against the jet-black jade of forest.

As Far As We Can See

Noon's coin thumbed in the air,
                              we sons lift back
the metal plates in the ground: each thin
metal vase raising from its missile silo one spiked flower,
the daylily or the yellow spatterdock, the homunculus flame

above the watery dissolve of as far as we can see.

As if all the dead were ours,
we dress them in wreaths of forsythia,
                              bright stone bouquets,
but, like the rain that shatters light into shards
of beryl & tourmaline, our children betray us,
don't they, Mom, the way the weather is always changing

to whatever it is . . . , your delicate bones
like branches beneath snow—then bonemeal, cornmeal, dust?

At your funeral at St. Joseph's,
the underflesh of umbrellas pounded back increments of rain—
the flowers dashed on stone
                    the way a pestle grinds scent
against the bone socket of the mortar your father brought
from Dublin: more an eyecup than a bowl.

                    Is this the stingy fragrance
the tiny violet stirs in the hairs of the nose
so sweet the scent is lost almost as we name it

the way, moments after you died, as the telephone
began its awful screeching—the amethyst sliver
of my contact lens sinking in the swimming pool—

I lost my sight in the surfeit of sun on water
and didn't think to move?

Anniversary

From where I kept myself from you
while you were living

the jumbo jet tears north through the nowhere
where you are now,

skeins of lightning through the clouds
like beaded reticules

spilling their privacies across a sky I can't get to.
And, even if I could,

my fears would drop in like commandos,
blood washing a killing floor

in the middle of nowhere, as if eternity
were so spartan & inarticulate

no amount of wasted breath could fill it
the way, when we open a window at the back of the house,

the song sparrow's song suddenly stops
—a disquietude, which also sings.

The White Sky

One sharp gold arrow to excite,
                    one blunt one, lead-tipped,
to repel, this is the nature of love, two arrows.

So flew the god & the virgin—
the one in desire, the one in dread.

But Daphne's father is a river god
so the earth beneath her swallows,
                        her feet struck hard,
the disheveled hair the shiny leaves of the laurel.

This is how the spirit world saves her from itself.
But you, Mom, are ravished into thin air

the way Agnes, the virgin saint you were named for,
runs out of miracles—a dagger in the throat

and she's *sponsa Christi,* like you
married to this impossible white sky.

So why did you lay down with man
and bear him all these. . . .

Apollo feels the flesh tremble beneath the bark.
The impatiens I prop on your stone in the morning

is blown by noon.

Blue Exorcism

This voice, a noon, can't be added to.

I wanted to say that the blue jay in the pear tree
is finally & momentarily still,
wing-feathers come together across the back:
a blue stained glass window.

Someone hopeful might imagine the martyr
taking each blue arrow, each blue undulation of the bowstring

inside the body, till he is a superlative form of blue,
like the ocean swell lifting a child-size you

out to sea, till Memory, that blue largess,
                                    tosses you back.
When even time betrays—holding back
its memorialized surf, its ebb & flow

of blue—you must look deeply into a human face
or look away.